BUSTARD

LEGENDS
&LEAGUES

or, Mr. Tardy Goes From Here to There

THIS BOOK
is dedicated to my grandparents,
Edwin & Agnes Bustard
—who, in their day, were quite the
WORLD TRAVELLERS.

NED BUSTARD

THE ILLUSTRATIONS
FOR THIS BOOK WERE A
COLLABORATIVE EFFORT
BETWEEN MATTHEW CLARK
AND NED BUSTARD

Veritas Press

Copyright ©2004 Veritas Press
www.VeritasPress.com
ISBN 978-1-932168-23-5

Third impression February 2010

Printed in State College, PA, U.S.A.

"PARDON ME, GENTLEMEN, but could you help me? I seem to be a bit lost."

"Please enter, my good man! You have come to the right place. Knowing how to get from *Here* to *There* is our specialty.

Allow me to introduce myself— I am Mr. Longitude, and my wide friend here is Mr. Latitude."

4

"Thank you so much for troubling yourselves. My name is Elmo Tardy. I seem to be always losing my way, and therefore I am always late. Today, for example, I have an appointment at . . ."

"Wait! Wait!" Mr. Latitude interjected. "I find it best not to begin with where you want to end up, but to first find out where you are."

"I'm right here," said Mr. Tardy.

"Of course you are," said Mr. Latitude. "But if you want to get to places like New York, Paris, or Cairo, you have to know more."

"But I'm just going—"

"Indeed," Mr. Longitude added, "your true location can only be known by where you are in relationship to other things. And the best thing for that is a map."

"A nap?" asked Mr. Tardy. "No, no, I don't have time for that. My appointment is—"

"No, not a nap—a *map.* Maps are useful things that have the big things around us drawn in small, simple pictures. A map can be made to show any place you want—from the things on your kitchen table to the entire world. There are maps of the bottom of the ocean and the stars of the night sky."

"I once tried to make a map that drew everything the same size that it was, but I couldn't carry it around," mumbled Mr. Latitude. "That's when I learned that maps aren't the same size as the places they picture. Big places are drawn small. The difference between the big, real place and its size on a map is called *scale*."

"What do maps look like?" Mr. Tardy asked.

"They come in all shapes and sizes," answered Mr. Longitude. "There are big maps and little maps, flat maps and round maps. There are city maps and country maps, maps with words and maps with symbols. And there have even been woven and carved maps."

12

"Why don't we show you how to use a map to travel to your destination?" suggested Mr. Latitude. "When using a map, the first thing you need to know is which end is up."

"But my appointment—"

"Yes, yes, in a moment," acknowledged Mr. Longitude, "but this next part is important."

13

"Most maps have something called a compass drawn on them that shows direction and has at least four points showing which way is North, South, East and West," instructed Mr. Latitude. "North is at the top of a map and refers to the North Pole—the tip top spot on our world. The bottom of the compass points south to the South Pole, the very bottom of our world."

14

"East and West are the other points of the compass. East is where the Sun comes up in the morning, and West is where the Sun goes down every night," said Mr. Longitude.

"We use North, South, East and West to give us the big picture of where we are going, but there are other things on a map that help us, too," Mr. Longitude said.

"Oh yes," Mr. Latitude began with excitement, "some of my favorite things on maps are the elegant lines that run around the world from East to West—called parallels."

17

"I've never seen any lines like that when I've walked around outside," Mr. Tardy said with a puzzled look on his face. "I think I would have noticed huge lines stretching from—what did you call it—East to West?"

18

"Oh, you don't see them because they aren't really there. They are only drawn on maps," chuckled Mr. Latitude. "There are also imaginary lines that run from North to South—aren't there, Mr. Longitude?"

"Indeed there are, Mr. Latitude," twinkled Mr. Longitude. "Though some lines are more important than others. For example, the most important parallel is called the Equator."

"The Equator runs around the middle of our world like the belt on my trousers—" Mr. Latitude illustrated, "dividing the world into the Northern and Southern Hemispheres."

Mr. Tardy looked skeptical. "Maps don't seem very useful if they are just full of imaginary things."

"Oh my dear Mr. Tardy, maps are full of real things, too—even if they are drawn teeny tiny," replied Mr. Longitude.

"The largest real things on maps are called Oceans. That is the name for the water at the Beach," continued Mr. Longitude. "In between the world's four oceans are giant piles of land called Continents."

"Continents are the seven biggest pieces of land in the world. Continents are filled with important things that show up on maps."

"First you find Countries, which are invisible, but everyone lives in one. Their borders are invisible lines that show up on a map," said Mr. Latitude.

"More imaginary things!" exclaimed Mr. Tardy.

"Don't worry, imaginary things don't take up much space. Then, some countries are divided up into smaller areas called states, provinces or territories."

"Are these smaller areas imaginary too?" asked Mr. Tardy.

"States are quite real," answered Mr. Latitude. "It's their border lines that are imaginary."

"In the land part of maps you will come across other real things like Mountains, Valleys, Hills, and Rivers. Mountains are very high parts of the land, and Valleys are very low parts," instructed Mr. Longitude.

"Hills are small mountains, and Rivers are like roads of water cutting through the land. Speaking of roads, they are on many maps as well. They are often the quickest way to get to places," said Mr. Latitude.

"Roads are more imaginary lines, right?" asked Mr. Tardy.

"Quite wrong," Mr. Latitude laughed. "Roads are real lines on the land."

HISTORIC ROUTE
NEW MEXICO
U.S.
66

"On road maps there are often big or famous things called landmarks. Little symbols mark these on a map to help direct us around," added Mr. Longitude.

"You keep talking about going around our world like it is a ball. As far as I have ever seen, the world is flat," protested Mr. Tardy.

"Indeed, Mr. Tardy, you are not the first to think that the world is flat," responded Mr. Longitude. "Yet the world we live on is actually round like a ball. It is called a globe. And a man named Ferdinand Magellan proved this back in the year 1519 when he sailed all the way around it."

"Our round world is so big that when it is lunch time here, it is the middle of the night on the other side. And we are not on the inside of the globe but walking on the outside of it. Yet in spite of the world being a globe, many of our most useful maps are flat."

30

"Maps can tell you how high places are and how far away one thing is from the other. Some maps will tell you how many steps to take, some how many feet apart places are, and many tell you how many miles separate one spot from the other."

Mr. Tardy looked at his pocket watch and jumped. "I really must be going. Will you unroll one of your maps to show me where I need to go?"

"Certainly," said Mr. Longitude. "What is your destination?"

Mr. Tardy replied, "I have an appointment with Dr. Bettertoo—my optometrist."

"How convenient," beamed Mr. Latitude. "His office is just next door."